FAMILIUS

Published by Familius LLC, www.familius.com
Familius books are available at special discounts for
bulk purchases for sales promotions or for family or
corporate use. Special editions, including personal-
ized covers, excerpts of existing books, or books with
corporate logos, can be created in large quantities for
special needs. For more information, contact Premium
Sales at 559-876-2170 or email orders@familius.com.
Reproduction of this book in any manner, in whole or
in part, without written permission of the publisher is
prohibited.

Library of Congress Cataloging-in-Publication Data
2016938727
Print ISBN 9781942934820

Printed in the United States of America

Edited by DeAnna Acker
Cover design by David Miles
Book design by Adam Eastburn

10 9 8 7 6 5 4 3 2 1

First Edition

TEACHERS'

LESSONS LAST A LIFETIME

(OR AT LEAST UNTIL THE NEXT EXAM)

175 *Jokes*

to last until
your pension

GENE & LINDA PERRET

Teaching is neither an occupation nor a profession; it's a vocation. Occupations and professions pay better.

Teaching is trying to get people who steadfastly refuse to listen to hear. Those nonlisteners could be students, or they might be parents. There's a good chance they could even be members of the school board.

Teaching is also trying to build tomorrows for people who would rather not be there today. Outside of an occasional apple on the desk or a maudlin, poetic note in the yearbook, teaching seems to be a thankless job. But it's not, really. The thanks are built into the job itself.

When a student learns despite lack of confidence or even outright resistance, that's thanks to the teacher. When a youngster with no direction suddenly transforms into a leader, the kudos belong to the person in the front of the room. When a child with no future reaches a goal, it's the teacher who deserves the gratitude. And when an unreachable tomorrow becomes today's proud reality, it's due to the dedication of some teacher.

May this book serve as a thank you to those educators who believe, persist, and deliver.

Thank you, Teach.

Youngsters keep you humble.

A teacher told a student, "You know, I collect my salary whether you learn your lessons or not." The student's eyes opened wide and he said, "You get paid for doing this?"

Teaching is a tough job. There's the name-calling, the bullying, the cliques ... and then, of course, you also have the students to deal with.

TO TEACHERS,

a perfect student
is one who has an
open mind and a
closed mouth.

Teachers should be paid like athletes. Either that, or athletes should be forced to grade papers after every game.

Teachers spend their entire lives teaching. . .

and the rest of the time grading papers.

ATHLETES

make more money and are
more popular than

TEACHERS.

That's because they don't end the
game by saying, "There'll be a test
on this next Tuesday."

Those who can, do.

Those who can't, teach.

Those who don't give a damn are students.

The kids in class know all there is to
know about everything.
THE TEACHER KNOWS THE REST.

The teacher said, "I gave you a multiple-choice exam. What more do you want?" The students all said **"More choices."**

When a student gets in trouble, a teacher keeps them after school.

That's not fair; the kids misbehave and the teachers get punished.

I had one teacher

that was so

,

when we studied

the cavemen,

he knew them

all by name.

I spent the last year of high school telling my teachers that the dog ate my homework.

On graduation day, the school told me the dog ate my diploma.

One teacher chastised me for
a wrong answer on a test.

She said, "How could you get that
wrong? Everybody knows the answer
to that question."

I said, "Then why did you bother to put
it on the test?"

One teacher gave me a

minus 10

on my exam.

He said not only were my answers wrong, but some of them were wronger than they should have been.

The teacher asked, "What is four squared?"

The student said, "It's the first words in Lincoln's Gettysburg Address."

I got a

zero

on my latest
math test, which
showed some
improvement.
Last time,
I got a

minus
zero.

The first day of school:
when parents earn a bit of
rest and teachers earn
their salary.

All classes were difficult for me—even

lunchtime.

The roast beef

in our cafeteria was almost as tough as some of our teachers.

Some teachers aren't that smart.

One of them wrote a book on mathematics and all the page numbers were wrong.

A good teacher will believe
that your dog ate your
homework.

A great teacher will believe
it even if you don't own a dog.

The teacher's lounge
is where teachers can
relax and start acting
like students.

One of my
teachers is
especially tough.

Rumor has it that when she
grades papers, she wears a
black hood.

We teachers are not crazy,
but sometimes the children behave
better when we let them think we are.

I had one teacher who
was such a jerk,
his personality had to be
registered with the local
police as a

LETHAL
WEAPON.

ANOTHER TEACHER WAS
SO BAD TEMPERED,

he handed out several
lifetime detentions
without possibility of
parole.

We had one teacher who was disliked by everyone.

The school held a fire drill every time she went to start her car in the parking lot.

We had a very easy gym teacher.

I used to sweat
more during
geography exams.

I asked my class, "How much homework do you think is too much?" They answered in unison,

"ANY."

I blame my
trigonometry
teacher for
killing my dog.
I was trying
to get Lucky
to eat my homework
assignment and
he choked on
an isosceles
triangle.

Fair is fair.

If I have to do homework every night, then the teacher should have to come to my house on the weekends and help me straighten up my room.

TEACHERS SHAPE THE FUTURE,

which is also when the students say they'll turn their homework in.

My English teacher
made me what I am
today—

an unpublished writer.

Teachers are
hard to understand.

They're supposed to
teach us what we should
know. But on tests, they
ask questions about
things we don't know.

The teacher said,

"If you don't hand in your homework, I'll flunk you. If you tell me your dog ate it, I'll flunk you and the dog."

Teachers used to be very important . . .
until the smartphone came along.

Imagine—all the
hard work and effort
you put in to teach
students how to spell
correctly has been
replaced today with
spell-check.

Teachers taught
us more than

reading, 'riting, and
'rithmetic.

They taught us morals,
loyalty, character, and
dedication.

Of course,
today they have
an app for
all that.

The work teachers do pays dividends tomorrow, next year, and one hundred years from now.

Which, incidentally, is when I'll have my book report ready.

I went to a tough school.

If a kid missed class, he didn't need a note from his mother but rather from his parole officer.

There's always one troublemaker in every class. More often than not, it's the teacher.

I'm not saying I was a troublesome student, but my teachers didn't get a salary—

they got hazard pay.

Class—that's
where I kill time
between visits to the
principal's office.

Teaching is

tougher than being a guardian
angel. Guardian angels don't
have to deal with parents.

Teachers are guardian angels

who have the power

to send you to detention.

The teacher called
my parents

into school so many times,

they had a better
attendance record
than I did.

They say that education is for the future.

GOOD. . .

then I'll go to school tomorrow.

For graduation,
my class invited all
our teachers. . .

or, as we like to call
them, "the survivors."

Teaching is tough.

It takes almost as much courage to stand in front of a class full of students as it does to eat in the school cafeteria.

Monitoring the lunchroom is tough for most teachers.

When they serve biscuits and gravy, the food fights can be lethal.

The best way to break up a
fight in the school cafeteria is
for the teacher to threaten the
participants with

second helpings.

This one teacher was mean.

If you acted up in class, she didn't

send you to the principal's office—

she had you deported.

When a fight breaks out
between two kids,

**the teachers
break it up.**

**If two teachers
get in a fight,**

we let it go on and take the
rest of the day off.

One of my teachers was

ancient.

When we studied
Benjamin Franklin's
autobiography,

she showed us her
autographed copy.

Great teachers show
us what we can do
with our lives. . .
or what we have left
of our lives when we
finally finish all the
homework
they've given us.

There was one teacher that didn't trust anyone.

If you brought him an apple, he made you take the first bite.

There were only two teachers that I didn't care for during my school days. You were both of them.

You were the kind of
teacher who made playing
hooky worth the risk.

You always insisted that there be no talking in your classroom.

Unfortunately, you were teaching our debate team.

Once, you gave me
a bad grade for not
dotting my

i's and crossing
my *t*'s.

That seemed unfair,
since it was an
oral report.

With most students,
their hearing is

FINE;

their listening is

DEFECTIVE.

I don't know why you
insisted that I give
oral book reports.

**I used to get so nervous
that I would stutter.**

My report on *War and Peace*
took three weeks to complete.

As a teacher,

you taught me
right from wrong,
Whatever you said
was right; whatever I
wrote on the tests
was wrong.

THE FOOD IN OUR SCHOOL IS BAD.

The cafeteria smells the same as the boys' locker room.

My homeroom
teacher was so strict,
to this day,
I won't go to the
restroom unless I raise
my hand first.

You were a tough

disciplinarian.

You kept me after school
so often that my parents
rented out my room.

I don't want to say "I told you so," but since I got out of school, I've started my own business, raised three kids, and lived a happy and productive life, and I've never ever had to find the square root of anything.

You could have
marked some of my
answers on the
HISTORY EXAM
correct.

After all, the story of
ancient civilizations is
not something that's
carved in stone.

Yes, in Bible stories, I did list

Goliath as defeating David.

But I was going with

the point spread.

One teacher was

SO SCARY,

if you brought him an apple,
you made arrangements to
have it delivered by
a bodyguard.

Dear teacher,

when I was a child,

I wanted to be a teacher just like you. I wanted to mold young minds and impart wisdom just as you did.

I wanted to stand before a class and have a positive influence on the young. But then I got a job instead.

As a teacher,
you were my role
model when I was in
your class.

Thanks to your help,
since then,

I've raised my
standards.

Teaching may be the
noblest form of

self-defense.

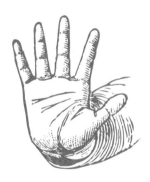

You flunked me in math, which inspired me to become what I am today—an IRS agent.

Teachers
and military
servicemembers
are the real
heroes of our
nation.

And both should
go through the
same basic
training.

Teacher,

the things you said in class were important. Sometimes, though, the things you didn't say at Parent-Teacher Night were even more important.

Teachers are nice people...
until the bell rings.

Teachers have it easy.

They get to teach
things they know.

Students have it hard.
They have to learn
things they don't know.

One teacher I had was
so nice, her multiple
choice tests had only
one choice. . .

. . . I still got it wrong.

MY TEACHER

sometimes loses her temper. Is it a coincidence that it's usually when I'm around?

As a teacher, I prepared my students for life.

They prepared me for damn near anything.

Dear teacher,

because of you,
I became me.

Teachers are
wonderful.

A teacher taught
me that.

Teacher, I fought you every
step of the way.

Thanks to you,

we both won.

It's great to get to the classroom

and see all those bright and shining faces. Almost as great as when you send them home at the end of the day.

Every prominent
person will tell you
that teachers were
responsible for
their success.

BIG
SURPRISE.

It's hard to become
successful if you can't
read, write, or do
arithmetic.

Being a teacher is like
pushing a young bird out of
the nest. What a thrill it is
to watch them fly.

**Teachers are sent
from heaven. . .**
often to put their students
through hell.

Dear teacher, during my school days, you were my light at the end of the tunnel.

Why they built our school in the middle of a tunnel,

I'll never know.

My parents

were always crazy about you as my teacher. Of course, they spent more time with you than I did.

Teachers are always expected to break up student fights.

They are the Texas Rangers of the educational system.

Some teachers are old.

I had one
who taught
history from
memory.

Dear teacher, I look forward to seeing you at our twenty-five-year class reunion.

BUT I MUST

WARN YOU—

I still don't have all my homework done.

AS A TEACHER,

I believe in the theory of "no kid left behind." Although I did have a few that lingered for a while.

Harassment, intimidation, and bullying have become a major problem in schools—especially in the teachers' lounge.

I became a teacher for one reason and one reason only. . .

to find out what really goes on in the teachers' lounge.

The teachers' lounge
is a lot like

VEGAS.

What happens there
stays there . . . until some
newbie posts it
on Facebook.

The nice part of being a
teacher is that you get an
assigned parking space.

Now if only they'd pay enough so you
can afford to buy a car.

The food in our school is so bad

that students get sent
to the cafeteria for
punishment.

As a teacher, one often wonders:

Are the students being attentive and respectful because they like me, or are they just doing it for extra credit?

I was so bad in school,

I always had to bring a
note from my mother.

But it paid off.

I've amounted to nothing, but

my mother became a writer.

**Teachers instill
in us the love of
good books**

but give us so much
homework we don't have
time to read.

Those who can,

DO.

Those who can't,

TEACH.

Those who can't do either

get appointed to the school board.

I learn a lot when I'm teaching children.

I learn nothing at faculty meetings.

Teaching
is trying to get
kids who know
everything to learn
something that they
don't know they
don't know.

The teacher said,
"I don't believe
you. Dogs don't eat
homework."

The student said,
"They do if you roll
it up and hide it
in little pieces
of cheese."

As a teacher, sometimes my
favorite students are the
ones who are

ABSENT.

Today, they have something called "pupil-free days."

We had those, too, when I taught school. We called them "the weekend."

As a teacher,
I love pupil-
free days.

It's like going to
the dentist and he
calls in sick.

There are two types of pupil-free days: There are days when the pupils don't come to school. Then there are days when they do come to school but I ignore them.

It's easy to spot teachers on the first day of school.

They're the adults who aren't smiling.

I'm a teacher.
When someone says

"back-to-school clothes,"

I think

straitjacket.

At the beginning of the school year, teachers find themselves longing to be audited by the IRS. It's a perfect excuse for them to miss Back-to-School Night.

At Parent-Teacher Night,

one mother said, "I understand my boy hasn't been showing up for class."

I said, "Which boy is yours?"

She said, "I don't know. He rarely shows up at the house either."

I'm eternally grateful to
the math teachers
of the world.

**Without them, I could
have gone through
my entire life not
knowing what a
hypotenuse was.**

ONCE, FOR HOMEWORK,

the teacher told me to find the hypotenuse. I wasted a whole day at the zoo.

I'll give you an idea how old one of my teachers was. She had a

GLOBE

in her classroom that she got when she first started teaching.

It had only

ONE CONTINENT

on it.

Many schools now want to teach what they call "new math."

I don't know— the old math worked pretty well.

There's a saying: "If it ain't broke, don't fix it." Apparently, that applies to everything except math.

I had one teacher

that was so old,
when he started
teaching, old math
was actually new.

THE NEW MATH

is so confusing. I asked
my teacher if
2 + 2 = 4.
She said, "This year. Next
year, we'll have to wait
and see."

The school administrators decided that we should opt to teach the new math.

They said, "Let's try it for twelve months or a year, whichever is longer."

As a student, it doesn't matter to me—

old math,

new math,

core math—

I can flunk 'em all.

There are three kinds

of math teachers—

those who can
teach math

and those
who can't.

Many of my students have said,

"There is no reason why I should have to learn math."

I wish I could be there for their first IRS audit.

A teacher's

GOAL

is to teach the children
enough so they'll have
plenty of things to forget
for the rest of their lives.

AS A TEACHER,

I believe in homeschooling,
provided I get to pick the
students who will do it.

I want to educate each
of my students enough
so that when they've
forgotten everything
I've taught them,

they'll still know
something.

You were a great teacher. You taught me my ABDs.

I can't make all of my
students geniuses—

only the ones who stay
awake during class.

I just want all of my
students to pass
their exams.

Let their
next teacher
educate
them.

My biggest concern as a teacher is at the end of the week.

What do I do with all the lesson plans I have left over?

Teachers have to plan what
they're going to teach

and how they're going
to teach it.

Then they stand in front

of the class and teach

it while the students sit

there and text one

another saying,

"What the heck is she
talking about?"

Teachers have a lesson plan
on what they're going
to teach that week.

Students have their own
lesson plan on how much
they're going to learn
that week.

Since I'm a teacher,

I may spend my next
vacation in a
voting booth.

I want a place where no one under
eighteen is allowed.

During a fire drill, the PA system tells the students to "follow the instructions of your teacher." So I guess if I want the kids to do what I tell them, I first have to set the classroom on fire.

I had one

VERY OLD TEACHER.

She was very strict about

not talking in class. It would

wake her up.

FOR A TEACHER,

hall monitor duty is like being a
cowboy in the

OLD WEST

who is in charge of
orderly stampedes.

My students will forget
ninety percent of what I
teach them in math class,

but the remaining fifty percent should serve them well.

Sometimes all the students need in
school is a kind word.
So I always go out of my way to
try to find somone
WHO'S WILLING TO GIVE THEM ONE.

One student told me he didn't think I was fair. He said, "You always give me lower grades than the kids who study."

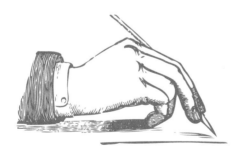

I always try to ask a few
really easy questions in
my classroom.

It's the only chance
some kids will ever get
to raise their hands.

What a teacher teaches a
child lasts for all eternity...

**or until the
next test,
whichever
comes first.**

My students know the lyrics to every popular song there is, but they can't remember the second sentence of Lincoln's Gettysburg Address. . .

. . . or even who delivered it.

My teacher taught me to respect history, to appreciate mathematics, to cherish geography, to admire the languages.

Now if she could arrange it so I could learn all those things without studying,

she'd really be onto something.

Teachers are unfair. On one math test, the question was, "How much is twenty-two plus fourteen?"

I wrote down "thirty-two," and the teacher marked that wrong. I should have gotten partial credit for coming closer than the rest of the class.

Anyone who thinks

we can't
change the past

has never seen the
answers my students put
on their history exams.

As a teacher, I like to give open-book tests. If nothing else, it teaches the students that their books

actually open.

I asked one student why he copied his test answers from the dumbest kid in the class. He said,

"So you wouldn't think I was cheating."

I told one student, "You got every answer wrong on your midterm exams."

He said, "That's your fault. Next time,

sit me next to a smarter kid."

I gave my students an

IQ test.

Half of them
misspelled it.

Years ago, *vocabulary* meant you helped the youngster learn new words in school.

Nowadays, it means helping them forget some words they've already learned at home.

I was always a
tough teacher.
When I taught
kindergarten,
I once gave a kid an
F in sandbox.

Once as a kindergarten

teacher, I said,

"Now it's nap time."

All the youngsters said,

"We don't want to take a nap."

I said,

"Who's talking about you?"

I'm not inherently a
mean teacher.

I'm just trying to
live up to the
nicknames
the kids think I don't
know about.

For every child that learns his lessons well, there are ten or twelve who want to sit next to him during the exams.

The good that one does as a teacher lasts forever. Sometimes it seems as though the school day does, too.

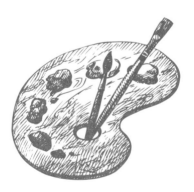

One teacher refused

TO RETIRE.

She has a walker that
would get to class before
she would.

How's this for a nasty teacher?

On the last day of school, he gave us

three months of homework.

How come

we teachers are
required to know
more than our
students

but we can't outsmart
any of them?

I teach creative writing. Well, I don't really teach it.

I just ask kids, "Tell me again why you were late."

You show me a teacher who can educate children without LOSING PATIENCE,

GETTING UPSET WITH PARENTS,

OR REBELLING AGAINST THE

SCHOOL BOARD,

and i'll show you a person who shouldn't be allowed in a classroom.

Your teaching
changed my life.
At least, that's what
my therapist says.

Our history teacher was so old,

the rumor around the school was that she dated all the fellows on Mt. Rushmore.

We had one teacher who we all thought had eyes in the back of her head.

Of course, a lot of her other body parts were in the wrong places, too.

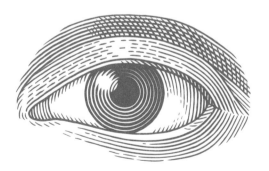

Being a teacher is a lot like being a lion tamer—

except in lion taming, you don't have to put up with parent-teacher conferences.

YOU

can't force-feed an
education to a child.
Although sometimes
we have to do
that with the food
they serve in the
cafeteria.

Teachers have to be creative—
especially during Parent-Teacher
Night when the parents ask,
"So, how's my child doing?"

One teacher was so tough,

no one ever brought
him an apple.
He preferred
raw meat.

All parents feel that their children should
get preferential treatment.

But fair is fair.

Parents of teachers think their children
should get preferential treatment, too.

A teacher must be

**COMPASSIONATE,
KIND,
CONSIDERATE,
GENEROUS,
COURTEOUS,
HELPFUL,
FAIR,
and RESPECTFUL**

Then when Parent-Teacher Night is over, she can go back to being herself.

When one student
understands the lesson,
that is the teacher's
ultimate reward. . .

or so I'm told.

May you teach
forever or until your
students finally
get it—

whichever
takes
longer.

Music teachers have an easy way of knowing when they've taught well.

They have their orchestra play the national anthem. If the audience stands up, it shows they were able to recognize the tune.

It's hard for us teachers to listen to the students'

oral reports on "What I Did Last Summer."

We're all too busy fantasizing about what we'll

be doing next summer.

You could be teaching
a future president of
the United States.

Teach so you'll
be invited to the
inauguration.

When you were my teacher,

you said that one day I'd be grateful for everything you taught me.

Well, I'm all grown up now, and guess what...

ABOUT THE AUTHORS

GENE PERRET has been a professional comedy writer since the early 1960s. He began his television writing career in 1968 on *The Beautiful Phyllis Diller Show*. Since then, he has written or produced many of television's top-rated shows, including *Laugh-In* and *The Carol Burnett Show*. During his career, Gene has collected three Emmys and one Writers Guild Award.

Gene also worked on Bob Hope's writing staff for twenty-eight years, becoming the comic's head writer and traveling to several war zones for Hope's iconic Christmas shows.

Today, he teaches classes in comedy writing. His hobbies include painting, sketching, and playing the guitar. He paints rather well and sketches adequately, but you don't want to listen to his guitar playing. No one does.

LINDA PERRET followed in her father's funny footsteps and sold her first professional joke in 1990.

Since then, she's supplied one-liners and comedy bits for Terry Fator, Wendy Liebman, Bob Hope, Phyllis Diller, Joan Rivers, Yakov Smirnoff, and other stand-up comics.

Linda was a staff writer for the television Emmy Award–winning special celebrating Bob Hope's 90th birthday: "Bob Hope—the First 90 Years."

She has cowritten two collections of business jokes, published by Prentice Hall—*Funny Business* and *Bigshots, Pipsqueaks, and Windbags.* She is the author of *HMOs, Home Remedies & Other Medical Jokes.* Her material has been quoted in *Reader's Digest,* the *National Enquirer,* and *Arizona Highways.*

Linda also launched a joke service called Perrets' Humor Files and continues to operate a newsletter for comedy writers and performers.

ABOUT FAMILIUS

Visit Our Website: www.familius.com

Join Our Family: There are lots of ways to connect with us! Subscribe to our newsletters at www.familius.com to receive uplifting daily inspiration, essays from our Pater Familius, a free ebook every month, and the first word on special discounts and Familius news.

Get Bulk Discounts: If you feel a few friends and family might benefit from what you've read, let us know and we'll be happy to provide you with quantity discounts. Simply email us at specialorders@familius.com.

www.facebook.com/paterfamilius

@familiustalk, @paterfamilius1

www.pinterest.com/familius

FAMILIUS

The most important work you ever do will
be within the walls of your own home.